Beating Heart Cadaver

by

Colleen Murphy

Playwrights Canada Press
Toronto   Canada

Beating Heart Cadaver © Copyright 1999 Colleen Murphy
Playwrights Canada Press
54 Wolseley St., 2nd fl.
Toronto, Ontario CANADA M5T 1A5
Tel: (416) 703-0201   Fax: (416) 703-0059
e-mail: cdplays@interlog.com   http://www.puc.ca

Playwrights Canada Press acknowledges the support of The Canada Council for the Arts for our publishing programme, and the Ontario Arts Council.

Graphic design by Arnold Koroshegyi.
Production photo by Nir Baraket.

Canadian Cataloguing in Publication Data
Murphy, Colleen, 1954 –
　　　Beating Heart Cadaver
A play
ISBN 0-88754-567-X
I. Title.
PS8576.U615B42   1999   C812'.54   C99-931069-7
PR9199.3.M824B42   1999

First edition: May 1999.
Printed and bound by Hignell Printing at Winnipeg, Manitoba, Canada.

Permissions

The following poems and extractions from poems are reprinted by kind permission of A.P. Watt Ltd. on behalf of Michael B. Yeats:

A Prayer for my Daughter	2 lines	prelims
Vacillation	full poem	page 10
Those Dancing Days are Gone	4 lines	page 36
To A Child Dancing in the Wind	full poem	page 45

From *The Collected Poems of W.B. Yeats*
Edited by Richard J. Finneran
Revised Second Edition
Published by Scribner Paperback Poetry
Simon & Schuster Inc.

––––––––––––––––––––

Connemara Cradle Song   page 81

By kind permission of Waltons of Dublin

Copyright 1950 Waltons Musical
Instrument Galleries Ltd.

2-5 North Frederick Street, Dublin 1, Ireland

Dedicated to Gladys Amelia McKean

"O may she live like some green laurel
Rooted in one dear perpetual place."

from **A Prayer for My Daughter**, W.B. Yeats

Colleen Murphy

Born in Rouyn-Noranda, Quebec, Colleen Murphy studied acting at Ryerson University and at the Strasberg Institute in New York. She writes for stage and film and twice won prizes in the CBC Literary Competition with *Fire-Engine Red* (1985) and *Pumpkin Eaters* (1990). She has directed three award-winning films, "Putty Worm," "The Feeler" and "Shoemaker." *Beating Heart Cadaver* is her third play. It was nominated for a 1999 Floyd S. Chalmers Award. Colleen Murphy resides in Toronto with her husband and son.

Author's Notes

The titles of the scenes are there to express the feeling of the scene, nothing more.

Covered in blood, Amelia exists in Leona's imagination and must be rendered with uncompromising physical boldness, otherwise she is reduced to sentimentality.

Acknowledgements

I wish to thank Richard Rose for his tenacity, the actors and actresses who shared their ideas — both in workshop and in production — and I especially wish to thank Maggie Huculak and Maria Vacratsis for their conviction.

I also wish to thank the Ontario Arts Council and Necessary Angel Theatre Company for their assistance in the development of this play.

Foreground: Victor Ertmanis, Maggie Huculak
Shadow: Tess Benger

Beating Heart Cadaver was first produced by Necessary Angel Theatre Company at the Canadian Stage Company in Toronto, on January 22, 1998, with the following cast and crew:

LEONA	*Maggie Huculak*
DANNY	*Victor Ertmanis*
AMELIA	*Tess Benger*
DEVLIN	*Kevin Bundy*
MIN	*Joyce Campion*
LOLA	*Maria Vacratsis*

Director	*Richard Rose*
Set and Lighting Designer	*Graeme S. Thomson*
Costume Designer	*Theresa Przybylski*
Sound Designer	*Todd Charlton*
Stage Manager	*Marinda de Beer*
Production Manager	*Mark Callan*
Music Director	*John Millard*

Characters

LEONA   30s or early 40s

DANNY   late 30s or 40s, Leona's husband

AMELIA   8, Leona and Danny's dead child

DEVLIN   mid 20s, Danny's brother

MIN   60s, Leona's mother

LOLA   50s

Scene 1

Let Grief Be A Falling Leaf

> *A wrecked car and a refrigerator are strewn along a road flanked on one side by woods. A chalk outline of a little girl is drawn on the pavement near the wreckage. Toys are scattered around. Wearing a black dress and carrying bulging garbage bags, LEONA enters from the road. Sensing something, she stops.*

LEONA   Amelia? *(calling softly into the emptiness, careful not to fracture the air)* Are you cold? Did you come in through the back door? I age when you do this, honey. Mommy's cell structure takes a beating every time you hide, mommy's chromatin fibres split open unravelling DNA which leaks into my bloodstream ordering my body to give up, because stress is the silent stalker you can't see can't hear 'til it creeps up behind you and carves off the side of your face. Did you know that? Amelia? Shall I tell you a story? This is a story about our future. Did you go into the cupboard? Poor little bug you must be starving. Wanna hot dog?

> *MIN enters. She wears a black coat.*

MIN   I thought you were going to take a nap.

LEONA   You frightened me.

MIN   Sorry. You should have come to the cemetery. Father Shea said a prayer and that was that.

LEONA   She's hiding again.

MIN   The parish will spring for a stone with a white baby lamb on top. Father pointed one out to me. White, cute — maybe too cute, but it's better than a plain grey slab.

LEONA   She's hiding under the couch, I bet.

MIN   Probably not, Leona, but why don't we check? *(looking under a piece of wreckage)* She might have been there but she's gone now.

LEONA   Where would she go? She should be in school. Maybe she's upstairs drawing pictures.

MIN   She's in heaven.

LEONA   No, she's wandering through another dimension, her body decomposing, her mind a total blank — no sorry, you're right, she's . . . maybe she's in the kitchen.

MIN   I'm getting a heart condition, Leona. Angina. Palpitations.

LEONA   I heard her singing.

MIN   My hair turned white overnight, now it's falling out.

LEONA   I heard her loud and clear, as if she's in the room.

MIN   She's in heaven with the angels and she's
          staying there! Now let's have tea before I
          faint from exhaustion.

LEONA   I'm taking these down to the Salvation
          Army.

MIN   It's too soon to be giving her stuff away.

LEONA   There are children out there who have
          nothing. Nothing.

          *LEONA exits. MIN peeks into the
          garbage bags and pulls out two Barbies
          and a naked Ken doll. LEONA enters
          with an armful of dresses.*

LEONA   Put them back in the bag, mom.

MIN   I'm keeping the Barbies I gave her, plus Ken,
          plus Barbies mobile home and the jeep.
          Where's Ken's tuxedo?

LEONA   *(snatching the dolls from MIN)* I'm taking
          them all down to the Salvation Army.

MIN   No, you're not! I'm keeping the ones I gave
          her. And the dresses — you can't just go
          giving the dresses I made her to complete
          strangers. They're not yours to give.
          (grabbing at the dresses) The blue crushed
          velvet one and the one I made with those
          happy face buttons, those are mine — and the
          green one with puppies on it, that's mine too!

LEONA   *(grabbing a dress from MIN)* This one's mine.
          I bought it on sale — it was ten regular
          thirty-something.

MIN   You're gonna regret tossing these out and
         regret is like cancer because it mostly gets
         worse. Which yellow one did I make her?

LEONA   The one with the white lace collar.

MIN   I'd like it back please and thank you.

LEONA   It's not available.

MIN   I loved that dress and want it back in my
         possession!

LEONA   You can't have it.

MIN   Why not?

LEONA   Because she was wearing it!

         Silence.

MIN   I never did like those sleeves on it, not fussy
         about puff sleeves ' the best of times.
         (pulling up anoth   dress) Now this is
         pretty. Who g ⸱ her this?

LEONA   Danny — an .t's for sure going to the Sally
         Ann.

MIN   He might want to keep something of hers.

LEONA   *(snatching the dress from MIN)* No.

MIN   I'm trying to be patient, Leona. I know you're
         suffering more than me because you're the
         Mother. I'm just the Grandmother, the
         sentimental favourite at birthday parties,
         but we take a back seat at disasters.

LEONA   *(reaching into the bag, she pulls out a green dress with puppies on it and hands it to MIN)* Here, keep the one you made her.

> *MIN puts her face into the dress. LEONA gathers up toys, crayons, hair bands, Barbie clothes and shoves them into bags.*

LEONA   And four or five years from now don't ask for little keepsakes or any sort of bathtub ducky because they'll all be gone tomorrow. Tomorrow they'll be assimilated into someone else's life . . .

> *LEONA picks up a threadbare teddy bear, looks at it for a moment, then tosses it into the bag.*

MIN   Don't give Binky away.

LEONA   . . . someone else who can wake up in the morning and know that if their spouse drops dead or if they discover their breasts are full of tumours it will not matter, for they will still find meaning in life, because even if their child is wearing some dead girl's dress and cuddling some dead girl's dolly, their child *lives*. Everything goes, her bed, bureau, snowsuit, mittens . . .

> *A tiny voice — childlike and hollow — begins to hum "Oh, How Lovely . . ."*

MIN   Danny will have fits of rage when he finds everything gone.

LEONA   . . . slippers, pyjamas, crayons . . . hear that?

MIN	All I hear is my heart racing and the roots of my hair separating from my scalp.
LEONA	Shhh.
MIN	*(listening)* What?

The humming evaporates.

LEONA	Nothing.

LEONA picks up the garbage bags and exits. MIN follows. As darkness falls a tiny voice drifts in from the woods.

AMELIA	*(singing)* "Oh how lovely is the evening, is the evening, When the bells are sweetly ringing, sweetly ringing, Ding, dong, ding, dong, ding."

Scene 2

"Since the lovely are sleeping, Go sleep thou with them"

LOLA, a big, happy lady, enters with a briefcase and a handful of pamphlets.

LOLA	Hi, I'm Lola Howe, founder and president of P.O.Y.A.V.O.C. — Parents of Young Accident Victims of Canada.

MIN enters wearing an apron over a flowery dress.

MIN	*(furious)* Get out!

LOLA   I'd like to offer you a one-year membership
            which includes free admission to our annual
            blow-out fundraiser —

MIN   Get out or I'll kick your shabby rump from
            here to Christmas. Living off the back of
            another's sorrow — have you no shame?

            *MIN shoves LOLA out. After a moment,
            DEVLIN enters carrying a large suitcase
            and pink hoolahoop. He is handsome,
            awkward.*

DEVLIN   Hello?

MIN   And who the hell are you?

DEVLIN   Devlin.

MIN   *(pause, then recognition)* Devlin Finn. I
            wouldn't have recognised you if you'd fallen
            on me. Thought you were another curiosity
            seeker. Come on in, don't be shy, make
            yourself at home.

DEVLIN   Nice to see you again.

MIN   *(calling)* Leona. *(to DEVLIN)* You've grown
            up or something. Dyed your hair? No, it's
            the weight. My god, you've lost a lot of
            weight. Well, I'll fix that. Sit down.

            *LEONA enters wearing a light coloured
            dress.*

LEONA   Devlin?

MIN   *(to LEONA)* The man near gave me a stroke.

DEVLIN   Hello, Leona. Sorry it took so long.

LEONA   I didn't think you'd got my message. The girl
          who answered the phone sounded drunk.

DEVLIN   How are you?

LEONA   Fine. Min's been staying with me, holding
          everything together.

DEVLIN   Terrible sorry about Danny. *(reciting)*
          "Between extremities Man runs his course; A
          brand, or flaming breath Comes to destroy All
          those antinomies Of day and night; The body
          calls it death, The heart remorse. But — "

MIN   I don't know why you're kicking up such a fuss
          about Danny — there's a seventy-five percent
          chance he'll recover.

DEVLIN   Sorry? I was under the impression he died.

MIN   No, no, it was Amelia who passed on.
          Danny's coming home today.

DEVLIN   Today? Christ, she balled the message up
          quite severely.

LEONA   It was Amelia's birthday so Danny drove her
          up to visit Min.

MIN   Excuse me, I've something on the go in the
          kitchen.

          MIN exits.

LEONA   On the way there a truck smashed into them.
         I was here. Amelia's friends were coming
         over for cake so I, I, had to bake the cake. I
         put it in the oven, set the timer —

         MIN enters holding a fancy cake and
         singing loudly, "For He's a Jolly Good
         Fellow."

LEONA   Mom, what are you doing?

MIN   Let's practice up. *(singing)* "For he's a jolly
         good fellow".

         LEONA joins in the singing.

MIN   "For he's a jolly good fellow, for he's a jolly
         good fellow " — Where's that lovely voice,
         Devlin? This is a happy occasion — a
         celebration of sorts, right, Leona?

LEONA   Of sorts. *(to DEVLIN)* I was here. Amelia's
         friends were coming over for cake so I, I, had
         to bake the cake. I put it in the oven, set the
         timer, finished decorating —

MIN   It's important we force ourselves to be happy,
         if only for a moment.

DEVLIN   I'll do my best.

LEONA   I was here. Amelia's friends were coming
         over for cake so I, I, I HAD to make the cake.
         I put it in the oven, set the timer, finished
         decorating then took a nap. The phone rang.
         It was Min wondering where Danny and
         Amelia were. If only I —

DANNY   *(off)* ANYBODY HOME?

> *MIN begins to sing. LEONA and DEVLIN join in.*

**MIN,
LEONA &
DEVLIN** *(singing)* "For he's a jolly good fellow, for he's a jolly good fellow, for he's a jolly good fellow, that nobody can —"

DANNY *(off)* HELP ME UP THE STEPS.

> *MIN exits. LEONA and DEVLIN continue singing. Loud banging is heard. DANNY enters, dragging himself along the ground like a seal. MIN enters behind him, pushing a wheelchair.*

LEONA Welcome home, Danny.

> *DANNY looks at up LEONA. There is a long silence between them.*

MIN "Although the world is full of suffering, it is full also of the overcoming of it." Helen Keller. Quotables from Notables.

DANNY Devlin, what are you doing here?

LEONA I thought you were dying so I called someone from your side of the family.

DEVLIN Sorry about what happened, Dan. How are you feeling?

DANNY   Grand. *(hauling himself into the wheelchair)* The quadriceps in my legs are a bit shrivelled but the doctor said I'll be walking soon. The feeling's come back into my arms and torso. Pinch me here, Leo.

LEONA pinches him.

DANNY   Harder. Hard as you can.

LEONA squeezes his flesh.

DANNY   OUCH. See, I felt that.

MIN   I baked you a cake, Danny.

DANNY   Thanks, Min.

MIN   It's a welcome home cake I baked especially. Can I cut you piece?

DANNY   Thanks, not right now.

LEONA   Let's have a drink. *(to DANNY)* Would you like a whisky?

DEVLIN   I've some duty-free.

DANNY   I can't have alcohol with the pills.

LEONA   Do you have pills?

DANNY   Yeah, anti-depressants. Mellaril, Parnate, Ipratropium, Tranylcypromine, Zoloft and another kind I can't pronounce. *(to DEVLIN)* And when did you creep in?

DEVLIN   Just now.

LEONA   He thought you were dead.

DANNY   I'm not dead, okay, Leo?

MIN   Will you have some cake now, Devlin?

DEVLIN   Later.

LEONA   Maybe Devlin can build a few ramps. One outside and one —

DANNY   I don't need damn ramps, Leo. This is a temporary thing.

DEVLIN   Anyone care for a drink?

DANNY   Sure. A double.

LEONA   You're not supposed to drink.

DANNY   One won't kill me.

DEVLIN   Good for the circulation.

LEONA   *(to DANNY)* Have you tried Phenobarbital?

DANNY   I don't know — how's it spelt?

LEONA   I'm taking it.

DANNY   What for?

LEONA   Severe anxiety, insomnia, depression.

DANNY   That makes two of us.

MIN   I've also been feeling blue. As the grandmother I'm carrying quite a load of sorrow and guilt.

DANNY   That makes three. *(offering MIN a pill)*
           Would you like something to cheer you up?

MIN   *(taking the pill from DANNY)* Sure, I'll try
           one.

DANNY   Gobble a few down, Devlin, they'll put hair
           on your brain stem.

DEVLIN   Never mix, never worry.

DANNY   I read a lot about brain stems. *(swallowing
           more pills)* There, I'm ready now.

MIN   Shall I cut you a piece?

DANNY   No, not cake. I'm ready to see the
           photographs.

LEONA   What photographs?

DANNY   Of, you know, the wake, the fu-fu . . .

LEONA   I don't have photographs.

DANNY   Didn't you take any?

LEONA   No.

DANNY   *(to MIN)* Did you?

MIN   You know how I am with cameras —
           everything comes out lopsided.

DANNY   *(to LEONA)* You mean there are no
           photographs of her fu-funeral.

MIN   We had the camera but Leo broke down when that truck driver showed up. Brought his whole family — took up half the pews.

LEONA   That man should have died.

DEVLIN   Was he drinking?

MIN   No, he was taking a fridge to his parents outside Toronto.

LEONA   A decent, hard-working non-drinker drives into Danny for no apparent reason. I wanted to peel the skin off his face, destroy his children —

MIN   That's enough now.

LEONA   You try taking pictures, Danny — you try pointing the camera at a shiny white coffin.

         Silence.

MIN   I sure hope somebody changes their mind about this cake for I'm tired of holding it.

DEVLIN   I'll have a piece for breakfast, I promise.

DANNY   Are you staying here?

DEVLIN   Sure, if you don't mind.

DANNY   *(to LEONA)* How did you find him?

LEONA   I picked up the phone.

DANNY   When?

LEONA   Day after the accident.

DANNY   And you just showed up now? What'd you do
          — swim?

DEVLIN   I was occupied.

DANNY   Occupied, sure — up to your eyeballs in
          savages and their friends.

MIN   We'll have none of that talk, Danny.

DEVLIN   I'll get a motel room.

DANNY   Nah, stay — what the hell. Can't find it to
          visit us 'til tragedy strikes then you show up
          with the booze and the restrained manners.

LEONA   *(to DEVLIN)* Come on, give us a tune.

DANNY   Give us a weeper.

MIN   Sure, I'm in the mood for something sad.

LEONA   "The Butcher Boy."

DANNY   Not that christly thing, Leo.

LEONA   It's very sad.

DANNY   There's a difference between very sad and
          tragically, pathetically morbid. Give us
          something melancholy.

MIN   "Carrickfergus."

DEVLIN   *(singing)* "I wish I had you in Carrick — "

DANNY   I HATE THAT SONG.

DEVLIN   How about the song I'd planned to sing at her
          wedding?

DANNY   Don't go singing anything dirty.

DEVLIN   No, nothing dirty, nothing happy, just
          something which leaves an aching void in
          the listener. *(singing)* " 'Tis the last rose of
          summer... "

DANNY   I HATE THAT SONG.

LEONA   Never mind, it's sad.

MIN   Sadness slows my pulse rate down to nothing
          and that's not a bad thing.

DEVLIN   *(singing)* ". . . left blooming alone. All her
          lovely companions Are faded and gone,"

          The others join in singing, voices
          straining, out of tune.

ALL   *(singing)* "No flower of her kindred, No
          rosebud is nigh, To reflect back her blushes,
          Or give sigh for sigh."

DANNY   *(raising his glass)* To Amelia Florence
          Kathleen Finn, dead at eight. May she sleep
          in the clouds, forever young.

MIN   "Sometimes, only one person is missing, but
          the whole world seems depopulated,"
          Alphonse de Lamartine, Quotables from
          Notables, under A, for absence.

DEVLIN   *(singing)* "I'll not leave thee, thou lone one,
          To pine on the stem; Since the lovely are
          sleeping, Go sleep thou with them."

MIN   Here's to the cakes she'll never eat.

           The tiny voice can be heard faintly
           singing "Oh, How Lovely . . . "

DANNY   To the wedding she'll not have, the man
           she'll not marry, books she'll never read,
           songs she'll never —

LEONA   Shhhh . . .

DANNY   What?

LEONA   Do you hear singing?

MIN   Leona, please.

DANNY   Yeah, Devlin was singing. I was singing, you
           were singing, we were all friggin singing.

LEONA   SHHH.

DANNY   Give yourself a shake.

           But the voice has faded into the air.

LEONA   I heard her.

DANNY   Who?

MIN   Ah, Danny, the good die young but the perfect
           ones leave even earlier and can you blame
           them? What with neglect and famine, what
           with babies suffering beatings and poor dear
           girls abducted into sex slavery then their
           stomachs slit open while they're still alive
           so their spleens can be removed and sold.

LEONA   *(to MIN)* Shut up.

MIN   I say get out while the getting's good.

DEVLIN   (*singing*) "So soon may I follow, When
              friendships decay,"

              *Everyone begins to sing again, except
              LEONA.*

ALL   " . . . And from love's shining circle — "

DANNY   Hold it. Bring down the photograph albums
              and her toys.

LEONA   Why?

DANNY   So we can have a proper wake for those of us
              who missed it — a proper wake right here in
              the bosom of her family.

              *LEONA looks at MIN for a moment, then
              exits.*

DANNY   I'm so relieved we took photographs. Up and
              down the CN Tower half a dozen times, out to
              the Santa Claus Parade, out to whatever
              kiddy thing was on the go, snapping
              photographs like maniacs.

LEONA   (*off*) This is way better than a photograph.

              *LEONA enters holding a balloon on a
              string, cradling it as she would a infant.*

LEONA   It's all I have left of Amelia. She blew it up
              before she got in the car that afternoon,
              remember? Her breath is still in here.

DANNY   Where did you get that thing?

LEONA   A policeman found it stuck in a tree and was kind enough to bring it here. I gave him five bucks. Do you want to hold it?

DANNY makes a grab for the balloon.

LEONA   Careful, you'll bust it.

DANNY   Gimme that thing.

He tries to puncture it with his fingers.

LEONA   What's the matter with you?

DANNY swipes at the balloon, hitting LEONA.

MIN   Stop it!

DANNY   GIVE ME THAT BALLOON!

DANNY tries to push himself to his feet but collapses back into the wheelchair.

MIN   Party's over. *(to LEONA)* Put that balloon away before someone gets hurt. *(to DANNY)* You can fight all you want with your wife but when you take a swipe at my daughter I'll not hesitate to introduce the back of my hand to your face, even if you are a cripple. I'm going home.

LEONA   You can't leave, mom. It's dark out there — it's NIGHT.

MIN   I spent all day baking a cake and no one even tasted it.

DEVLIN   Cut us a slice, then.

DANNY   I DON'T WANT ONE BLOODY PIECE OF THAT WOMAN'S CAKE!

MIN   *(to DANNY)* No one asked you.

LEONA   Someone might be hiding in the back seat.

MIN   Nice seeing you again, Devlin, though under such tragic circumstances.

DEVLIN   Pleasure.

MIN   Goodnight, Leona. Call me everyday.

LEONA   Check and see if anyone's hiding in her car, Devlin.

MIN   Leona, for the love of God —

LEONA   You might be followed, mom — caught in sniper cross-fire, struck by lightening. You might run out of gas near King City at exactly the same moment an escaped killer sees your car lights and afterwards all that's left of you is a handful of hair. This is a fact, a fact of life.

DEVLIN   Perhaps I will have a quick look in the back seat.

> *MIN and DEVLIN exit. LEONA exits with the balloon and enters again without it.*

DANNY   What will you call me? Handicapped, afflicted, disabled?

LEONA   I'll call you Danny.

DANNY I missed you, Leo. Why didn't you come visit me?

LEONA I did. Once. The day it happened. A nurse took me into Intensive Care so I could see you were still alive under all that equipment and my god, you were. Then Min went to the morgue and . . .

    Silence.

DANNY Do you want a divorce?

LEONA Why would I want a divorce?

DANNY It happened so fast. We were singing then I, CRUNCH . . .

    The sound of a car crash, a thump then shattering glass.

DANNY She, she, she, awwwwwwwwwwwwww . . .

LEONA Shhhh, everything is going to be fine.

DANNY I crawled over to her. She was lying on the pavement, leg bent back under her —

LEONA Don't tell me the gory parts, I never want to hear them.

DANNY I administered Cardiopulmonary Resuscitation but it was too late — she died instantly.

LEONA Thank god.

DANNY If she hadn't died instantly I could have saved her, Leo, I could have.

LEONA   Thank-what's-left-of-god Amelia did not
          suffer.

DANNY   But if if if if if if.

LEONA   Shhhh. We're going to start all over again,
          Danny. Just you and me. Just the mommy and
          the daddy.

DANNY   I'm a thousand times sorry, forgive me.

LEONA   There's nothing to forgive. It was an
          accident. One minute you're standing up, next
          minute you're lying down. Accidents happen.
          (pause) Danny? Maybe she didn't die.
          Maybe she got up off the pavement all by
          herself and walked away. She walked down
          the road and disappeared into the woods —
          now she's lost. Yes, it was someone else's
          little girl who was buried that morning.
          Danny? I think that's what she's been trying
          to tell me lately. To look for her — to find
          her.

          *But DANNY is asleep. LEONA looks up
          and sees the shadow of a little girl, her
          small arms waving. Darkness falls.*

Scene 3

The far distant shores of life.

> DANNY *languishes in his wheelchair.*
> LEONA *sleeps on the wreckage.* LOLA
> *enters.*

LOLA   Hi, I'm Lola Howe, founder and president of
P.O.Y.A.V.O.C — Parents of Young Accident
Victims of Canada, and you are . . .

DANNY   Danny Finn. This is my wife, Leona.

LEONA   Pleasure.

LOLA   Mr. and Mrs. Finn, I'd like to offer you a one-
year membership which includes free
admission to our annual blow-out fundraiser.
What'd you lose? Arm? Leg? Was she/he a
son, daughter, teenager, pre-pubescent,
infant?

LEONA   Our eight year old daughter.

LOLA   You poor aching human beings. Never mind
perusing our brightly coloured pamphlets, just
join up because let me tell you, you're about to
begin an intimate and necessary relationship
with pain.

DANNY   Pain is the only thing I actually feel any
more, Mrs. Howe.

LOLA   Call me Lola and I'm glad you feel something
because you've a lifetime of suffering to look
forward to. Now sit down and tell me about
your loss then I'll tell you about mine.

LEONA   The day of Amelia's eighth birthday, Danny
         drove her to visit my mom. On the way there
         a truck smashed into them. Truck driver
         was fine, Danny was seriously injured but
         Amelia . . .

LOLA   A tragedy.

LEONA   We're still waiting for the insurance report.
         The truck driver may have fallen asleep.
         He'll be charged with negligence.

LOLA   You weren't in the car?

LEONA   No, I was — it was her birthday and her
         friends were coming over for cake so I, I HAD
         to make the cake. I put it in the oven, set the
         timer, finished decorating then took a nap.
         The phone rang. It was Min wondering where
         Danny and Amelia were. If only — if if if
         only I'd been in the car this never would have
         happened.

DANNY   How do you know?

LEONA   I would have seen it coming.

DANNY   Bullshit.

LOLA   I do the odd bit of palm reading myself.

DANNY   It wouldn't have made any difference if you
         were there or not.

LEONA   Oh, yes it would have.

LOLA   My analyst says reality is indifferent but I
          think horrifying things happen because of
          something we've done. One too many
          abortions, stolen things in the past, secret
          hatreds — behind the terror hides the wish.
          We fulfil our destinies.

DANNY   The man was tired, working two jobs — you
          think he drives into me to fulfil my destiny?

LOLA   Yes. Your destinies collided.

DANNY   Gimme a break.

LOLA   Her time was up.

LEONA   It was not! I only had her for 416 weeks
          which is 2,912 days which equals 69,888
          hours which comes to 4,193,280 minutes or
          251,596,800 seconds. I miss her. I want to be
          with her. Sometimes I hear her singing . . .
          (calling out into the woods) Amelia . . . ?

LOLA   You're me all over again. I wanted to jump
          into my son's grave — still do.

          *Deep in the woods, the shadow of a little
          girl is seen moving.*

LEONA   I have to find her. *(calling)* I'm coming, pet.

DANNY   Get a grip — we've got company.

LEONA   *(to DANNY)* SHUT UP. *(then, gently)*
          Amelia? *(climbing over the wreck towards
          the shadow)* See, she's right in front of me.

DANNY   EARTH TO LEO.

        LEONA puts her hand out towards the shadow, but it is disappearing into the woods.

LEONA   *(inconsolable)* Oh, she's going . . . she's gone . . .

LOLA   "Your children are not your children. They are the sons and daughters of Life's longing for itself. You may house their bodies but not their souls, for their souls dwell in the house of tomorrow, which you cannot visit, not even in your dreams." That's our mantra, Mrs. Finn, "Your children are not your children, your children are not your children".

LEONA   If, if, if, only I had — but it was her birthday. Her friends were coming over for cake so I HAD to make the cake —

LOLA   Okay, my turn.

LEONA   I put it in the oven, set the timer then —

LOLA   IT'S MY TURN.

        LOLA opens her briefcase to reveal a garish lighted shrine to her dead son, complete with electric candles and a photograph.

LOLA   He was ten. I remember it like it was yesterday though we are talking eleven years ago. I have spent every moment since in an endless, eye sucking search for why. I got through the who, what, where, when, but stumbled on why — why why why why?

DANNY   I can relate.

LOLA   A single-celled suction cup could relate, sir.
        Strong, fairly plump, rigid people *melt* after
        hearing about Donald, also known as Donny.
        I call him Donny because that conjures him up
        as younger. I mean he was young — ten — but
        Donald makes him a jot more sophisticated
        then he actually is, was, is, was. Donald
        Joseph Howe. A veritable Olympian in the
        making. Donny's future lay in gymnastics.
        Double jointed, I tell you that boy was
        plasticine.

LEONA   I don't want to know what happened to him.

LOLA   Tough! He was in the school yard at lunch
        time, nothing extraordinary that day but a
        peanut butter sandwich lurking in the lunch
        bag of young piss face, Alistair Roden
        McBride, nine years old and I'll not forgive
        the fucker save today he might be dying of
        AIDS or catching a hearty dose of the flesh
        eating disease hundreds of miles from any
        penicillin in a car with four flat tires and no
        spares! Oops, sorry.

            LEONA exits.

DANNY   *(calling)* Leo? Leo? Come back here.

LOLA   Sorry. Lost my cool — a minor outbreak, it
        won't happen again.

DANNY   I think you should leave, Mrs. —

LOLA   It seems they were having their lunch outside
        at the end of the field that day. The lunch
        lady, Hazel, let them do that on occasion.
        She was a well meaning half blind gal who
        oversaw four hundred day kids eating
        staggered lunches, so a chance to let a few

LOLA   *(cont.)* boys out of her hair was a welcome to her. Alistair McBride, Billie Popper, Moe King and Donny took their lunch bags across the field and I guess Alistair got an idea to tease Donny — and that was my only child, Mr. Finn, all that would ever be for I was forty-one at the time.

DANNY   I think you should go.

LOLA   I was at work at the telephone company, when the principal called. "Go to North York General Hospital, Mrs. Howe, quick RUN," he said, "Donald's taken a terrible turn." The principal neglected to tell me Donald was already dead. I should have sued the school. Not a day goes by my heart doesn't vibrate with regret.

DANNY   What happened to him?

LOLA   At the beginning of the year parents filled out forms stating allergies, etc., and they were to be handed out to all staff. Two months later they were still sitting in the janitor's office in the brown bag they were collected in. Principal's secretary forgot to pass them out to the teachers, a Miss Staples — I'd like to staple her eyes shut.

DANNY   What happened to Danny? I mean, Donny?

LOLA   And Staples had the gall to apologise. I should have put a contract out on her life, or better yet, shot her myself, over and over again.

DANNY   Mrs. Howe, how — how did whatever happen happen? They were eating lunch?

LOLA   Well, it seems they were having their lunch outside at the end of the field that day. The lunch lady, Hazel, let them do that on occasion. She was a well meaning half blind gal who oversaw four hundred —

DANNY   You've told me that part already.

LOLA   Let me see. Alistair, Billie, Moe, lunch bags. Okay, lunch bags. I was at work at the telephone company when the principal — I'm lost.

DANNY   How can you be lost in your own story?

LOLA   I have it memorised in a particular order.

DANNY   Can't you just tell it in your own words?

LOLA   So-so-soon you-you won't be able to tell your story in your own words either, Mr. Finn, because you'll have processed a version which will protect you from the shivers and addict you to the tears. In fact, I'll bet you've already fashioned a mythology of idealisation and vilification so isolated from yourself —

DANNY   Get out.

LOLA   You're just jealous because my story's better than yours.

DANNY   GET OUT!

LOLA   My story's better than yours because it has more SUSPENSE.

> *She exits. DANNY wheels over to woods and calls . . .*

DANNY   A-a-amelia?

> *He waits. LEONA enters.*

LEONA   *(calling softly)* Amelia?

DANNY   Don't say her name any more, Leo.

LEONA   *(chanting softly)* Your children are not your children, your children are not your children, your children are not your children . . .

> *AMELIA's voice rings through the darkness.*

AMELIA   *(singing)* "Oh how lovely is the evening, is the evening, When the bells are sweetly ringing, sweetly ringing, Ding, dong, ding, dong, ding."

Scene 4

vanish: disappear suddenly; disappear gradually, fade away; cease to exist.

> *Sporadic hammering can be heard as DANNY lolls in the wheelchair parked in front of the TV. A flickering headlight shines on the wreckage.*

TV VOICE An open pneumothorax occurs when there is a penetrating wound to the chest and air is going through the wound into the pleural space. It is called "open" because the pneumothorax is "open" to the outside through the wound. A sucking chest wound is an open pneumothorax. Air can also enter the pleural space from inside the body through a damaged lung or airway.

> *He turns off the TV.*

DANNY Leo? *(waiting)* Leona? I'M STARVING!

> *DANNY notices something on the ground. It is one of AMELIA's broken crayons. He picks it up then looks for more. DEVLIN enters, carrying a hammer.*

DEVLIN Come outside, see what I'm building.

DANNY Don't grab me like you're grabbing a box of fries off the counter!

DEVLIN Sorry. I thought you'd like to participate.

DANNY I'm participating by breathing.

DEVLIN   It'd be helpful if you tried the ramp, see it's
          not too steep.

DANNY   Try one ramp, you tried them all.

DEVLIN   Don't give up hope. "Hope is the risk that
          must be run."

DANNY   Is this the part where you look me in the eye
          and say in your slow, always musical
          whimper, "You . . . can . . . walk . . . "

DEVLIN   That's hardly what I meant —

DANNY   Pinch me. Pinch me hard — right here.

          DEVLIN pinches him.

DANNY   HARDER.

          *DEVLIN squeezes very hard. DANNY
          pushes his hand away.*

DANNY   What do you know about hope?

DEVLIN   I can try and squeeze even harder.

DANNY   *(mimicking)* "Hope is the risk that must" —
          is that what you think when you hurl a bomb
          into the street?

DEVLIN   Fuck off.

DANNY   And if it explodes on some poor bum carrying
          groceries home —

DEVLIN   Fuck off.

DANNY   Are you thinking far into the future then or
        does the future only belong to Irish Catholics
        — especially the ones from Canada with the
        fake Irish accents —

DEVLIN Build your own ramps if you're so fucking
        capable.

DANNY   I saved your life once or have you forgotten?
        Driving along the beach road I see a figure
        bobbing up and down, and something in the
        way the arms were fluttering made me stop
        and rush into the water with all my clothes
        on and there you were, eh? So I grabbed you
        and you surfaced — wheezing, latching onto
        my neck like a horrible bloodsucker and I'm
        trying to hold you up but you're slipping
        away screaming "help, I can't touch bottom"
        screaming like a, no you're not — who was
        screaming?

DEVLIN I wasn't screaming. It was you were screaming
        your throat out.

DANNY   I never had time to scream, I was too busy
        rescuing you from a watery grave. Tilt head,
        open airway, take deep breath and seal your
        mouth around casualty's mouth. Pinch
        nostrils and blah, blah, blah. I still know it
        off by heart.

DEVLIN Stand up.

DANNY   Eh?

        *In one single move, DEVLIN hoists
        DANNY up to his feet and holds him.*

DANNY   Holy god — I felt that. I felt my quads tingle.

DEVLIN   The body remembers.

DANNY   Eh?

DEVLIN   In the 18th century, Stephen Hales, a Brit clergyman, tied a ligature around the neck of a frog and cut off its head. The heart continued to beat. Thirty hours later the limbs of the animal still withdrew when stimulated. Involuntary reflex action. Come now, *(stamping his feet in time)* "Come, let me sing into your ear; Those dancing days are gone, All that silk and satin gear; Crouch upon a — "

DANNY   Ah, Devlin, if that young girl was still among us we'd all be sane. I'd be at work, you'd be in a grotty bar singing the glories of a Protestant slaughter, and right about now Leona would be picking up that same young girl from Dover Public, and that young girl's hair would be sparkling in the sun and all would be right in the world.

LEONA   *(off)* DANNY, COULD YOU COME UP HERE?

DANNY   *(calling)* Sure, and I'll take the stairs two at a time!

        DEVLIN helps DANNY back into the wheelchair. LEONA enters, somewhat dishevelled looking.

LEONA   Sorry, I forgot.

DEVLIN Hi, Leona.

LEONA I saw the ramps from the window. They look good.

DEVLIN Yeah, they'll work fine.

DANNY Didn't you hear me calling?

LEONA I was on the phone.

DANNY I'm starving to death.

LEONA You could have made yourself a sandwich.

DEVLIN I'm going around the corner. Do you want anything, Leona?

LEONA No thanks. Well sure — chips, chocolate bars and a couple bottles of whisky.

DEVLIN exits.

LEONA I just talked to the lawyer, Danny.

DANNY Where's the rest of her crayons? Where's Binky?

LEONA Pardon?

DANNY Binky.

LEONA Binky? I . . . I sent Binky out to the dry cleaners.

DANNY Why? I want to smell her smellies on it, the ten thousand kisses she gave that stupid thing — I WANT TO SMELL HER.

LEONA   The truck driver isn't going to be charged, Danny.

DANNY   Why did you send it to the — never mind. Gimme a couple of her dollies to hug.

LEONA   I gave away everything she owned, Danny.

DANNY   Eh?

LEONA   Everything's gone. Everything.

DANNY   Even her dollies?

LEONA   Dolls, everything, even her shoes.

DANNY   But . . . why?

LEONA   The day of the funeral I heard rustling in her room. She was up there.

DANNY   Give yourself a shake, Leo — god, you're scaring me.

LEONA   I heard her breathing hard as if something was caught in her windpipe. It got on my nerves so bad I packed up everything she owned and, Danny, I meant to take it all to the Sally Ann, I even borrowed Min's car and was almost there when this urge to throw everything out overtook me and . . . it's not at the dry cleaners. Binky's in a dumpster behind a strip mall along Kingston Road.

DANNY   Kingston Road?

LEONA   But she's still here, Danny — she's looking for me.

DANNY   She's DEAD.

LEONA   I know, but —

DANNY   No you don't, Leo. You think she's still
             running around here like an itchy leprechaun
             but she's dead — dead, dead, dead, dead.
             *(disgusted, he tosses back a handful of
             painkillers)* What colour was the dumpster?

LEONA   I can't remember. Grey, maybe blue.

             DEVLIN enters with a bag.

DEVLIN   They didn't have any bars but I got crisps
             and —

DANNY   Devlin, could you help us find Binky?

DEVLIN   Sure. Who's Binky?

LEONA   Amelia's teddy.

DANNY   DON'T SAY HER NAME!

DEVLIN   What's the thing look like?

DANNY   Like this . . . *(yanking a photograph from his
             pocket, other photographs tumbling out)*
             Oops, shit. *(looking down at a photograph)*
             Light brown fur, one missing ear, one cracked
             eye — I can't bear to look . . .

             *DANNY pushes the photograph at
             LEONA who looks at it for a second.*

LEONA   I can't bear — get it out of my face!

> *DEVLIN takes it then slips it in his pocket. LEONA's attention is caught by another photograph. Her whole body lights up.*

LEONA . . . that's the day we bought Amelia blue cotton candy then took her up on the ferris wheel . . . look.

DANNY Don't say her name!

LEONA *(scooping up the photograph, laughing)* Look . . . look at her.

> *She shows it to DANNY, and for a moment they forget everything.*

LEONA Her mouth's covered in blue sticky guck and those eyes, look — she always looks right at you, doesn't she? *(suddenly snatching up the photographs)* You must never touch these.

DANNY HEY —

LEONA Oil from your fingers will cause deterioration. They must be kept in air-tight conditions or they'll disintegrate within two hundred years.

DANNY Then let's enjoy the damn things while they last.

LEONA Everything is vanishing, Danny.

DANNY Yeah, and you're speeding up the process. Tossing all her stuff away — have you lost your fucking brain stem?

DEVLIN There's no need for this kind of —

DANNY   You killed her off, you symbolically killed
         her —

LEONA   *(throwing the photographs at DANNY)*
         LOOK WHO'S TALKING.

DANNY   SHUT YOUR FACE.

DEVLIN   Calm down — both of you.

DANNY   *(to DEVLIN)* GET OUT OF THIS ROOM —
         GET THE HELL OUT OF THIS ROOM.

DEVLIN   Fine. I'll go to the movies.

         DEVLIN exits. Silence.

LEONA   If you'd taken the route we normally took
         instead of that godforsaken concession road in
         the middle of nowhere. If —

DANNY   I WAS IN A RUSH — you said be back at
         three o'clock, and I would have been if —
         what do you mean he's not gonna be charged?

LEONA   The tire marks on the road were — why
         didn't you tell me?

DANNY   What?

LEONA   You crossed into the path of the truck, not the
         other way round.

DANNY   I crossed, yeah — I crossed to get out of his
         way!

LEONA   That's not what the insurance —

DANNY   I WAS THERE, LEO. They were sitting in some office building in downtown Toronto but I was there experiencing the experience of flying glass and twisted . . .

>   *The sound of a car crash rumbles through his head. He covers his face.*

DANNY   Do you not believe me?

>   *Silence.*

LEONA   Was her seat belt on?

DANNY   It was on — of course it was on.

LEONA   Are you positive?

DANNY   Her seat belt was on, I swear it was, I remember fastening it.

LEONA   Are you sure?

DANNY   IT WAS ON . . . but she might have pulled it off when we were singing — you know how wiggly she gets, especially when she's excited.

LEONA   When that happens I stop and help her put it —

DANNY   IT WAS ON. She was in the back. We were singing, laughing and for one brief shining moment I thought I'd better make sure she's buckled up, so I asked her.

>   *Silence.*

LEONA   And? What did she say?

DANNY   We were having so much fun, I, I don't know.
I can't remember.

LEONA   You've remembered every sports score for the
last thirteen years, don't tell me you can't
remember this . . . this most . . . this most
significant . . .

> *LEONA pulls a bottle from the bag
> DEVLIN brought in.*

DANNY   Everything is vanishing. First that young
girl, then the sensation in my body and now
you. Where are you going?

LEONA   To bed.

DANNY   Please, Leo. Lay down beside me, just for a
minute or two.

> *Silence. DANNY opens a bottle of pills
> and swallows a handful. Darkness.*

Scene 5

Come peer into the darkness to see those who have gone before.

> *LEONA's flashlight sweeps across the darkness. The balloon is tucked under LEONA's arm. The silhouette of a young girl, AMELIA, can be seen — then it disappears.*

LEONA Amelia? Did you know when someone dies in a family, a door is opened? This door cannot be shut. It remains ajar, beckoning, tantalising us with the unknown, appealing to our curiosity. "Come closer," it says, "Come peer into the darkness to see those who have gone before." Are you hiding again, Amelia?

> *She sweeps her flashlight and the light passes over DEVLIN who is standing there.*

LEONA Christ god, you scared me.

DEVLIN Sorry.

LEONA What are you doing down here?

DEVLIN Nothing. Bad dreams.

LEONA Do you want some whisky?

DEVLIN No thanks.

LEONA It'll help you sleep.

DEVLIN Does it help you?

LEONA   Sure. No, nothing helps.

DEVLIN   I'm sorry I never met her, Leona.

LEONA   She would have liked to have known her uncle.

DEVLIN   I imagine she was quite sunny.

LEONA   Sunny's a good word.

DEVLIN   Was she musical at all?

LEONA   Yes. Loved to sing.

DEVLIN   May I hold the balloon?

LEONA   It's like an incubator. Her breath is still warm.

> *DEVLIN tosses the balloon up, tapping it, keeping it in the air.*

LEONA   Careful — you'll drop it.

DEVLIN   "Dance there upon the shore; What need have you to care For wind or water's roar? And tumble out your hair That the salt drops have wet; Being young you have not known The fool's triumph, nor yet Love lost as soon as won, Nor the best labourer dead And all the sheaves to bind. What needs have you to dread The monstrous crying of the wind?"

> *DEVLIN passes the balloon back to her. She takes it.*

DEVLIN   Yeats called nightmares "the horses of disaster."

LEONA   The first time I met Danny, he was dancing. I watched him for a long time then everything fell away when I realised he was coming towards me. I was so stoned . . . my underwear was soaking wet . . .

> *She swings her flashlight and the beam rests on DANNY, asleep in his wheelchair.*

LEONA   . . . it startles me that it took us five years to conceive a . . . sorry. I'm sorry.

DEVLIN   Nature is startling.

LEONA   Yes. Yes it is.

DEVLIN   Goodnight.

LEONA   Devlin, short of a miracle Danny will never recover.

DEVLIN   Never?

LEONA   It's a kindness to him not to pretend otherwise. Goodnight.

> *She flicks her flashlight off.   Darkness.*

Scene 6

Fill my pink lungs with oxygen.

> *DANNY is flopped in his wheelchair. MIN enters.*

MIN   Has everyone forgotten me?

DANNY   Min, Minnie. Minnie Mouse.

MIN   You're drunk.

DANNY   No, but cripes I gotta quit taking these pills. Want some?

MIN   Leona never called me. Someone could invite me to dinner. Roast beef with mashed, a mouthful of desert. I'm Amelia's grandmother.

DANNY   Shhh. No one's allowed to say her name in this house.

MIN   I don't give a fingerful of farts what's allowed — I'm Amelia's grandmother and I'll be her grandmother forever! I thought about her or was doing something for her or I'd drive down here — a day would not pass, Danny boy, that Amelia was not a very large part of. God forgive me for bringing this up but I hope you have another, if not my heart will give out from sheer uselessness.

DANNY   I'll do my best.

MIN   Three hundred years ago when I was a teenager the thought of babies disgusted me but at twenty I jumped into bed with anyone who hadn't dropped anchor and by thirty I'd met Robert and had Leona. She was a fine girl — bit plump, not brilliant — but she was mine. My peach-head, my luluhoop, my puffball. There were times I wanted to throw her against the wall and let her slide down in liquid form but mostly I adored her. When she married you I thought she'd left me but she came back the morning Amelia was born. Then I had two special girls. Today I have none.

DANNY   Same here.

MIN   Where is Leona?

DANNY   Upstairs. Sleeping. Passed out, probably.

MIN   And Devlin?

DANNY   Planting bombs in the downtown core.

MIN   I never put much stock in those rumours.

DANNY   What about me? I'll be your puffhead, your
          son-in-law, your cripple.

MIN   It's hard not to blame you — you're a lousy
          driver at the best of times. Hard not to hate
          your guts for what Leona's been through.

DANNY   Is it possible for you to put your arms around
          me because I . . . no one's hugged me since I
          came home.

          *MIN tentatively puts her arms around
          him.*

MIN   It's all my fault. If I'd never asked you to
          bring her over that afternoon, if if if.

DANNY   No, it's my fault.

MIN   It's my fault!

DANNY   It's mine.

MIN   It's mine.

DANNY   It's mine, mine, mine, mine.

MIN   All right, fine, it's yours! *(opening her purse and taking out a rolled-up bundle)* I've been carrying this around with me but I want you to have it now. *(pressing the bundle into his hand)* Don't let Leona see it or I'll be in the dog house for sure.

> *MIN exits. DANNY gently unfolds AMELIA's green dress with the puppies on it.*

DANNY   Amelia . . .

> *He holds up the dress, unable to contain his joy.*

DANNY   . . . I remember putting my hand behind your beautiful, tiny head, tipping it back just so, placing my mouth on you little lips and filling your pink lungs with oxygen . . . and oh oh you're perfect, just as when you were born and your face was all wet then you . . . o . . . o . . . opened your infinitesimal mouth and cried.

> *He presses the dress to his face.*

Scene 7

A state beyond coma.

DANNY and LEONA are in front of the TV, glued to the flickering light.

TV VOICE   Severe shock can develop after a casualty is released from the weight which caused the injury. When the crushing force is removed, fluids from crushed tissues leak into surrounding tissues causing shock. For crush injuries, give first aid for wounds and fractures while waiting for transportation to medical help.

DANNY turns off the TV. Silence.

DANNY   I'm starving to death. Where's dinner?

LEONA   You relish this, don't you?

DANNY   What?

LEONA   Barking out orders like a triple star general.

DANNY   Think I like being in this chair, day in, day out? Think I like having to ask for everything?

LEONA   Yeah, you do.

DANNY   You're right. Come on, gimme dinner, take me for a walk, get me a drink, suck my — SUCK MY COCK.

Silence.

LEONA   What do you want — rice or potatoes?

DANNY   I'm sick of rice. I want cream puffs, something sweet.

LEONA   We don't have cream puffs.

DANNY   You wish I died, don't you?

LEONA   Maybe there's cookies in the cupboard.

DANNY   Don't you?

          Silence.

DANNY   I'm a piece of wreckage that won't die and you can't stand it. That's why you never came to the hospital, eh?

LEONA   Don't GRAB at me —

DANNY   Say it.

LEONA   I wish.

DANNY   You wish WHAT?

LEONA   I wish it had been me who'd gotten smashed up then you'd see how it feels dragging around a useless lump, putting up with tantrums from a two-hundred-pound cripple who can't make himself a sandwich with his two good hands! Looking at me with that moony look as if I can feel anything short of disgust being touched by a man whose shitty bum bag I gotta manipulate.

          DANNY covers his face.

LEONA   You took away our child and eighty percent
         of yourself and fifty percent of me — MY
         FUTURE. Her and me and the possibility of
         anyone else — gone forever.

DANNY   I'm sorry.

LEONA   Sorry isn't good enough any more. I may as
         well have been in that car with you.

DANNY   Don't say that.

LEONA   Why not? I was in that car.

DANNY   No, you weren't — you don't know what
         happened.

         *LEONA pushes him hard and his
         wheelchair backs up. He grabs for the
         brakes.*

LEONA   Maybe I wasn't in that car, Danny, but I WAS
         IN THAT CAR.

DANNY   Hey!

LEONA   Gimme my wheelchair.

DANNY   Hey don't, you're tipping me over —

LEONA   Where's my wheelchair? I want MY
         wheelchair.

         *LEONA tips DANNY's wheelchair and
         he slides to the floor in a heap. She sits
         down in the chair and wheels around.*

LEONA   Wear a chair. They're all the fashion this season. Wear a chair slightly off the shoulder, running down the spine. I need a chair, Danny, because no one's comforting the real cripples — the ones with the marshmallow hearts who can't stand it any longer. *(breathing)* I'm so numb I don't know how my body remembers to breathe.

DANNY   You don't know what numb is.

LEONA   Surely there are different kinds of numbs.

DANNY   Numb, numb nuts, numb skull.

LEONA   Numb is numb.

DANNY   *(calling)* Devlin?

LEONA   He's probably at the movies.

> *DANNY crawls over to her, reaches up and gently caresses her foot. Slowly she withdraws it and wheels away.*

DANNY   Come here.

> *She does not move.*

DANNY   Come on, what the hell you think I'm gonna do — I'm your husband.

> *He lies down flat.*

DANNY   I'd make an interesting rug, eh? Lay me by a fireplace and hey — Danny the Rug. Lie down.

> *A moment, then LEONA gets up out of the chair and lies down beside him.*

DANNY   I should slap your face off.

LEONA   Do and I'll slap yours to pieces.

DANNY   Let me touch you.

> *Slowly, delicately, DANNY slides his hand up LEONA's skirt.*

DANNY   Remember our second date? Down at my folks' cottage? Remember you brought your stupid dog along, Whistle, was it Whisker, Whistle?

LEONA   Whisper.

DANNY   Right, and when Whisper wasn't barking extremely loud and making a fool of himself, he was eating my mom's laundry. Remember that?

LEONA   Yeah . . . your mom was funny about laundry.

DANNY   I'd be funny too if some strange dog was chewing my dirty clothes.

LEONA   Your mom was suspicious of me.

DANNY   How many times did I do this to you that weekend?

LEONA   A couple.

DANNY   How many?

LEONA   Lots.

DANNY   How many? Exactly how many times did I push my hand up you and all my fingers and make you cum.

LEONA   Ten, eleven.

DANNY   Fourteen times. And what did you say to me after every time?

LEONA   I . . . "Let's get married."

DANNY   You didn't say — I said that. I said let's get married. You said something else.

LEONA   I said "Do it again."

DANNY   Yeah, but no, after. Every time you caught your breath you'd say you couldn't wait for the real thing. Remember?

LEONA   Yeah. Yeah, I remember. *(breathing hard, she finishes)* Oh god.

DANNY   Well, this is the real thing now. *(holding her)* I can imagine how everything felt, Leo, but I feel nothing.

         DEVLIN enters. He carries a bag. One of his hands are bloody.

DEVLIN   Oops, sorry, I — I won't look.

DANNY   Christ, knock, eh.

LEONA   What happened to your hand?

DEVLIN   Nothing. Here . . . *(handing the bag to DANNY)* I thought you might like this.

DANNY   *(looking inside)* Binky? *(pulling out a dirty, crushed teddy bear from the bag and is thrilled)* Binky!

LEONA   You found it! Where did you find it?

DEVLIN   I went to five strip malls. Sorted through slime, slop and garbage. Nearly cut my arm off on a tin can.

LEONA   *(taking DEVLIN's hand)* Come to the kitchen and I'll disinfect it.

> *DANNY watches LEONA and DEVLIN exit, then he kisses and smells the teddy.*

DANNY   You look pretty rough, pal. Here, have a couple. *(opening his bottle and forcing pills into Binky's face)* Take the whole friggin bottle.

> *He throws the pills away, pulls more from his person and tosses them away.*

Scene 8

The horses of disaster.

> *Darkness. LEONA's flashlight passes over DANNY who is asleep on the wreck, clutching Binky. She takes Binky from him and dangles it in the air like a lure.*

LEONA   *(whispering)* Look who I found . . . Amelia? Come and say hello.

DEVLIN   Hello?

Her flashlight sweeps over to DEVLIN.

LEONA   Nightmares again?

DEVLIN   Yes.

LEONA   Amelia adored this old thing. *(absently twirling Binky around)* Inanimate objects sometimes absorb spiritual powers from their owners which protect — no, sorry, I don't believe that any more. I *(tipping Binky upside down)* That's funny . . . Binky's toes had little suede pads at the bottom, not vinyl. *(looking at Binky's face)* And his eye was way more . . . wobbly.

DEVLIN   I bought it new, Leona.

LEONA   Pardon?

DEVLIN   I bought it new. I pulled off its ear, just like in the photo, then dirtied it up. Scratched up my hand on purpose.

LEONA   Why?

DEVLIN   I wanted to contribute something.

LEONA   If you wanted to contribute something why didn't you go looking for the real thing instead of trying to trick us with this shitty imitation?

She throws Binky to the floor.

DEVLIN   I did, but the dumpster had been removed three months ago and the contents incinerated in the same week.

LEONA   Danny and I may be sad and desperate but
         we're a long way from stupid. At least I am.

DEVLIN   Please don't tell him.

LEONA   I'm going to bed.

DEVLIN   It's a recurring nightmare I get, Leona. I never
         actually toss the thing, but I touch the
         package as I pass it from one set of hands to
         another.

         LEONA stops.

DEVLIN   We watch the news. A child is injured in the
         explosion. About four he was, four or five.
         The blast blinds him, mucks up his brain.
         There wasn't supposed to be kids in the
         vicinity. There's never supposed to be people
         in the vicinity but where's making a big bang
         in a bloody void going to get you? I feel so bad
         I secretly sent him a train set, then a toy
         car — money once too. Then I get courageous.
         Sent him a bicycle which was too damn big
         and I had such a wrestle with it at the post
         that the clerk had time to recognise me.
         When my crew gets wind of me trying to stuff
         a bicycle down a mail slot, my telephone
         starts ringing . . . but I wake up. I always
         wake up, Leona. *(pause)* Goodnight.

         DANNY exits. When he has gone,
         LEONA passes her flashlight over the
         darkness and screams when she sees
         AMELIA playing with Binky. LEONA
         turns the flashlight off, then on again.
         AMELIA is gone. LEONA picks Binky up
         and tucks it in beside DANNY. As she
         does this, she notices AMELIA's green
         puppy dress sticking out from his shirt.

LEONA   What the heck is this? *(shaking him)*
Danny?

DANNY   *(groggy)* Eh?

LEONA   Where did you get . . .

> *LEONA tries to pull out the dress.*

LEONA   I'm going to kill Min.

DANNY   *(holding the dress back from LEONA)* It's
mine.

LEONA   *(trying to snatch it from him)* No it is not —
IT'S MINE.

DANNY   It's all I have left of Amelia.

LEONA   I want it back.

DANNY   Did you hear that?

LEONA   What?

DANNY   I said her name out loud.

LEONA   *(yanking the dress)* GIVE IT TO ME.

> *They both pull hard and the dress rips in
> half. LEONA and DANNY stare at
> what they have done.*

DANNY   I'll get a needle and thread.

LEONA   *(calling)* Amelia, your dress is here. *(pause,
then chanting)* Your children are not your
children, your children are not your children.

Scene 9

Your children are not your children.

> LEONA *is holding the ripped dress and
> the balloon. There is something lunatic
> in her stance. DANNY sits in his
> wheelchair watching her.* LOLA *enters.*

LOLA   Hi, you called?

LEONA   Sit down, make yourself at home, never mind
the mess, I've let the housekeeping slide.

LOLA   You were a car accident, right? Kid, right?
Died, right?

LEONA   It was her birthday and her friends were
coming over for cake so I, I HAD to make the
cake. I put it in the oven, set the timer,
finished decorating then took a nap. The
phone rang. It was Min wondering where
Danny —

LOLA   Yeah, yeah, I get the gist.

LEONA   I thought nothing of it — a traffic jam,
Sunday drivers. The second call came half an
hour later. I was in the tub. I thought it was
Min calling to say they'd arrived so I let it
ring and ring. It stopped, then started ringing
again. I dried off and picked up the bedroom
phone. It was the police. "Mrs. Finn, I regret
to inform —

LOLA   All right, thank you — NEXT — just kidding.
            You better get out of the house more often.
            Kick up your heels, visit the deceased's
            current residence, go shopping. Stay focused
            on your grief, Mrs. Finn. I visit Donny's grave
            three times a week — Mondays, Wednesdays
            and Fridays, twice on Sundays and holidays.
            I spend the rest of the time hanging around
            hospitals. Why, you ask? WHY?

LEONA   Why?

LOLA   I love Emergency rooms. I love the smell of
            iodine, the whoosh of life support machines,
            the bittersweet stink of oxygen mixed with
            urine — you can't beat that combo. And you
            can't beat the charged atmosphere — emerge
            doctors and anaesthetists hopping around the
            corridors like bunnies filled with a
            tremendously grim sense of purpose. All those
            sights and sounds help me remember the last
            chaotic moments with Donny when he was a
            physical entity, dead but still in one piece.
            They conjure up my last moments with him
            and that keeps me from jumping in front of a
            speeding car — oops, sorry.

LEONA   I can't remember Amelia's last moments with
            me.

LOLA   Sure you can. Hang around gas stations and
            you'll find yourself helplessly responding to
            the smell of gasoline and burning rubber.
            Memory exists, Mrs. Finn, so that we may
            have roses in December.

LEONA   I wasn't in the car, I never went to the morgue,
            I, I — I can't even remember saying goodbye.

LOLA   You're me all over again. It's a hell of a thing to be there when your child dies, but it's a trillion times worse not to be.

LEONA   My daughter died instantly.

LOLA   You lucky duck.

LEONA   What happened to your son?

LOLA   *(opening her briefcase, her perpetual shrine)* He was ten. I remember it like it was yesterday though we are talking eleven years ago. I have spent every moment since in an endless, eye sucking —

DANNY   Eye sucking suction cups — I've already heard that crap.

LOLA   Oh, Mr. Hospitality, you're awake — I thought you were catatonic.

DANNY   Get out of my house!

LOLA   All right, all right, you win — I'll tell it in my own words.

        Silence.

LEONA   *(to LOLA)* What happened to your son?

        Silence.

DANNY   Make it snappy!

LOLA   The, the, the health forms. (pause, then repeating) The health forms —

DANNY   Get to the point!

LOLA   The health forms didn't get to the staff so no
            one knew. That noon time, Al, Alistair was
            eating his p, p, peanut bu, bu, butter
            sandwich. Donny mentioned he was fa fa
            fatally a, a, allergic to such things. Al,
            Alistair probably took this as some kind of
            masculine dare and proceeded to shove his
            pea, pea, peanut butter sandwich down
            Donny's throat and there were no mommies
            around or supervisors or guardian angels in
            the trees to stop Billie and Moe joining in the
            fu fu fun and the mo mo, the more Donny
            heaved and convulsed, the more the boys
            laughed . . . *(whispering)* My dear Donny . . .
            every second of my life is shattered by what I
            imagine your last moments were without me.
            Every second is infused with the sound of your
            throat closing. At night I hear you
            (microscopic) "mommy, mommy", 'til the
            vowels have no room left to squeeze out.
            (pause) Don't pity me, Mr. and Mrs. Finn. I
            don't want your pity.

            LOLA exits.

LEONA   You're right, Danny.

DANNY   What?

LEONA   I wish you had died.

            *LEONA reaches her hand out towards
            AMELIA who is standing near a tree,
            bloody and unravelling. Darkness.*

Scene 10

Life is an incurable disease.

>*DANNY is parked in front of the TV. He is trying to properly wrap a triangular bandage around Binky's head.*

TV
VOICE   . . . bleeding from the scalp is often severe and may be complicated by a fracture of the skull or an embedded object. When giving first aid for these wounds, avoid direct pressure, probing and contaminating the wound. Apply a thick, sterile dressing that is large enough to extend well beyond the edges of the wound and bandage it firmly in place with a head bandage. If there is an embedded object, apply a large ring pad over the dressing to maintain pressure around the wound.

>*MIN enters carrying a brightly wrapped gift. She turns off the TV.*

MIN   I kept her birthday present. Mind you, she never got it so it's not really hers — but it's the thought. *(unwrapping the gift)* She'd enough Barbies to sink a ship so I put my money on a Spanish Dancer, flamenco, you know, with the red dress and the black lace, a very striking looking thing. Amelia would have gone wild for it. *(holding up the doll)* Now, here, isn't she a beaut? You can prop her up on your bed or tuck your spare roll of toilet paper under her dress.

>*She sits the doll on DANNY's lap. DANNY does not respond.*

MIN   I'll take you for your walk then buy you a muffin and coffee.

DANNY   I don't want any more muffins or cups of coffee.

MIN   Something more substantial? Roast beef with mashed? Pig on a spit?

                    With difficulty, DANNY pulls prescriptions from his pockets and hands them to her.

DANNY   Could you get these filled?

MIN   I thought you stopped taking pills?

DANNY   These are different.

MIN   *(reading)* Mellaril, Parnate, Ipratropium, Tranylcypromine, Zoloft —

DANNY   I had a wife who loved me, a child I adored. That was Danny not this — this helpless slug dribbling pee-pee and grief.

MIN   The paralysis is temporary, Danny — short term, fleeting, but life goes on. "Life is an incurable disease." Who said that . . . *(pulling out a book and flipping through it)* How about something under courage? "To see what's right and not to do it is want of courage." Or, "Cowards die many times before their deaths; The valiant never taste death but once." Shakespeare. I love Shakespeare.

DANNY   Please shut up.

MIN   Let's stick to hope . . . Emily Dickinson. Now I like her, listen, "Hope is the thing with feathers that perches in the soul, and sings the tune without the words —"

DANNY   SHUT UP. *(pause)* A hundred and twenty tablets of Mellaril will kill an adult male. This is a fact, Min.

MIN   It'll be a fine frosty Friday morning before I'll ever consider — What about Leona? What about MY baby?

DANNY   She'll find someone else. Someone with legs.

MIN   If you leave Leona, I'll haunt you. If there's such a thing as the living haunting the dead I'll drive you right out of the ground, Danny boy, and bring all manner of horror and torment upon your bones. If you give up on yourself, you've given up on Leona, and if you've given up on her, you've given up on me, and if you've given up on me . . . well then Christ, there's no one else to give up on.

DANNY   Please, Min. I can hardly lift my arms any more.

MIN   Sure you can. You lifted them up last week. Mind over matter. Come on, lift them up.

      DANNY barely manages to lift them up more than a few inches.

DANNY   I'm lifting them up.

MIN   Lift them right up over your head.

DANNY   I AM LIFTING THEM UP OVER MY HEAD.

> *Suddenly, MIN picks up the doll and
> tosses it high into the air. Involuntarily,
> DANNY reaches up to protect himself
> and catches the doll — his arms
> stretched high over his head.*

MIN   In a few years, if things become intolerable —
       god forgive me for saying this out loud — but
       when such a time comes I'll close my eyes,
       Danny boy, *(taking the prescriptions)* and
       remember what you told me.

DANNY Can I practice bandaging your head later?

MIN   Sure, just don't mess my hair too much or pull
       any of it out.

> *MIN wheels DANNY off.*

Scene 11

"Angels are coming to watch over thee."

> *LOLA sits on the wreckage. MIN enters
> wearing a bandage around her head.*

LOLA   Hi. What'd you lose — arm, leg,
       consciousness? Need a little consolation? Sit
       down, tell me your tragic tale and I'll tell you
       mine.

MIN   It's nothing. My son-in-law was practising on
       me.

LOLA   Is he a doctor?

MIN   You're that blood-sucking freak who gets off
       on accidents, aren't you?

LOLA   It's a living.

MIN   Leave me alone. I threw up this afternoon.

LOLA   I throw up every afternoon, twice on Sundays
         and holidays.

MIN   I have pains in my chest — cardiomyopathy,
         atherosclerosis.

LOLA   My carotid arteries are blocked so bad I suffer
         continuous transient ischemic attacks.

MIN   I've been diagnosed with involutional
         melancholia which includes delusions of ill
         health, sin, the non-existence of the world
         and preoccupation with death.

LOLA   How about a story to cheer you up? "He was
         ten. I remember it like it was yesterday
         although" —

MIN   I'm not interested.

LOLA   I don't blame you — Donny's story bores me
         stiff. I wish he'd been a cancer victim, a
         sickly boy who wrote poetry in between
         debilitating chemo treatments then up and
         died during the Christmas Party at Sick
         Kids — died right on Santa's lap — died
         choking on a candy cane. Cancer stories have
         sorrow built right into them and they're
         mercifully short. Mine's got suspense, sure,
         but plodding, I tell you there are days I don't
         know which part of the damn story I'm in or
         out of or who I'm addressing or what colour
         slip I put on that morning but — and here's
         the real heartbreaker — without that story,
         without that thin, trembling narrative, my
         life is incomprehensible, even to me.

> *MIN pulls out her quote book and flips through it.*

MIN And I quote, "Not the power to remember, but it's very opposite, the power to forget, is a necessary condition for our existence." Unquote.

LOLA What'd you lose — son, daughter, teenager, pre-pubescent, infant?

MIN My only granddaughter.

LOLA Sit down, tell me all about it then I'll tell you all about mine.

> *MIN sits down beside LOLA.*

MIN She had my hair and my jawline.

> *Darkness.*

Scene 12

The Breath of Life

> *LEONA enters wearing a dark coat.   She carries an old wreath and a shopping bag.*

LEONA   Amelia? *(sniffing)* I smell gasoline or . . . *(sniffing)* . . . is that diesel fuel? That's motor oil — that's STP motor oil, isn't it?

> *She sees AMELIA, bloody and hovering.*

LEONA   Why did you die? Why? You were having such a good life. The only bad thing that ever happened to you was the time you got lost at the Santa Claus Parade. Remember? I told you, "Honey, if you want to stand on the curb, stand where I can see your boots" — they were those orange rubber things you hated wearing. Fine, I kept my eyes on your boots, and you were very good about standing in one place, Amelia. It was hard with those three fat guys in front of me but I could hear you shouting at the clowns and pipers as they marched by. I knew I'd reach for you once the Santa float passed and, sure enough, the crowd started folding up, taking everyone into itself, including you. I couldn't see your orange boots, Amelia . . . ? Five hundred thousand people in parkas heading for their cars and AMELIA!

> *AMELIA exits.*

LEONA   Danny took off to get help. You couldn't have
gone far but my insides were doing
somersaults so I ran up to a policeman who
was wearing one of those red noses —
remember those spongy red noses? I had one
on, you had one, Danny did — I started
shouting at this policeman and his big red
nose bobbed at me "Lady, relax, every year,
500 kids disappear for a couple minutes — just
stay where you were." But the goddamn
noses, and oh, all the worse thoughts kept me
screaming at him then looked up across the
road . . . way on the other side and saw you
standing on top of a ladder, pointing, pointing
at me . . . as if, from out of this huge crowd,
you were asked to choose your parents and you
picked me to be your mother. I threw my
hand up over my head and waved — Amelia!
Then you smiled and pointed and I followed
where you were pointing and sure enough . . .

*DEVLIN enters, carrying a jacket. He
stops when he sees LEONA.*

LEONA   . . . there's Danny running through the park
pulling three policeman along with him, his
nose falling off and when he sees me I point
up towards you. Then he looked up and
screamed — it was a happy scream, Amelia
— and he ran over to the ladder, and I ran
too, and the gentleman who found you brought
you down and, oh honey, you were crying and
laughing, Danny was bawling, and I was,
well, I can tell you my chromatin fibres took
one hell of a beating that day . . .

*LEONA looks up at DEVLIN, aware for
the first time that he has been watching
her.*

LEONA   Where's Danny?

DEVLIN   Taking his walk.

LEONA   I went shopping then I walked to the cemetery. There's a little baby lamb on the top of Amelia's stone. I'm not fond of lambs — they're too fluffy. I would have preferred a plain stone or no stone at all. She must be terribly cold out there all by herself —

DEVLIN   Stop tormenting yourself, Leona. Let her go.

LEONA   Are you off to the movies again?

DEVLIN   Yes. Want anything while I'm out? Crisps, soda? Could I bring you back some popcorn?

LEONA   No thanks.

He moves to exit.

LEONA   Devlin, wait — could you do me a great favour?

DEVLIN   Bottle of Bushmill's?

LEONA   Sing "The Butcher Boy" for me.

DEVLIN   I'm not really in a singing kind of a mood.

LEONA   I read about a woman with three kids. They were hiking in the wilderness when a, a cougar sprang out and started mauling the little boy. The woman grabbed a stick and smacked it. She kept the cougar at bay so that the other kids could take the injured boy and get help. The kids met a man in a truck and he drove back to rescue the woman. But all he found was her jacket on the ground so he shouted into the woods. Then he heard the woman weakly asking if her kids were safe. I imagine her lying there, the cougar tearing at her chest, pulling at her eyes, lying there listening to that man's voice, listening to that voice coming from the far distance shore of life and shouting loudly that "yes, yes your children are safe." Then she died.

DEVLIN   *(singing)* "In Moore Street where I did dwell. A Butcher boy, I loved right well. He courted me, my life away and now with me he will not stay."

          LEONA begins to keen.

DEVLIN   *(singing)* "I wish my baby it was born and smiling on its daddy's knee, And my poor body to be dead and gone with the long green grass growing over me."

          LEONA keens loudly.

DEVLIN   *(singing)* "He went upstairs and the door he broke" *(stopping)* Perhaps I'll end there.

LEONA   No no, don't stop now.

DEVLIN   *(singing)* "And found her hanging by a rope. He took a knife and cut her down and in her pocket these words he found . . . Oh make my grave large, wide and deep, put a marble stone at my head and feet. And in the middle a turtle dove, so the world may know I died for love."

　　　　　Silence.

DEVLIN   I once walked into a lake. Singing at the top of my lungs and having a great commune with nature but my asthma struck and I started to sink. Danny came along, and don't ever tell him this, but when I saw him dog paddling towards me I was overcome with gladness 'til he started taking me out deeper. I kept screaming "you're going the wrong way, buddy", but he was drunk. Finally I got him turned round towards shore then I passed out. Next thing I was lying on the sand with his face slobbering all over mine. Apparently I'd stopped breathing and turned blue but it was Danny snatched me back from the brink, Leona. Danny saved my life.

　　　　　LEONA reaches up to DEVLIN.

DEVLIN   Do you want me to sing you another song?

　　　　　LEONA takes his face in her hands. They kiss, then kiss harder.

　　　　　After a moment, DANNY enters in an electronic wheelchair. He stops and watches them kissing. For a long moment, he watches . . . then DEVLIN senses something.

DEVLIN Sorry I, Christ . . .

> *DEVLIN scrambles to his feet.*

DEVLIN Excuse me.

> *DEVLIN exits. Silence.*

DANNY I desire you all the time now, did you know that?

LEONA Danny, don't.

DANNY Are you trying to make me jealous?

LEONA He sang for me and I . . . I felt released. That's all.

DANNY My baby brother releases my wife. It's a bad movie, don't go see it. *(calling up)* I SHOULD HAVE LET YOU DROWN, I SHOULD HAVE HELD YOUR FRIGGIN HEAD UNDER THE WATER.

LEONA I know what you're thinking, Danny.

> *DANNY notices the shopping bag and reaches for it.*

DANNY What's this?

LEONA Nothing. I went shopping.

> *She picks it up and holds it out of his way.*

DANNY All by yourself?

LEONA Yeah.

DANNY   Weren't you frightened?

LEONA   A little bit.

DANNY   What did you buy? Perfume?

LEONA   No.

DANNY   What's in the bag?

LEONA   Clothes.

DANNY   Your clothes?

LEONA   Yeah.

DANNY   Frilly night gowns?

LEONA   Sure.

DANNY   Crotch-less panties?

LEONA   I'll put these upstairs then make supper.

DANNY   You're not going up there until he comes down.

LEONA   I kissed him once.

DANNY   What's in the bag?

LEONA   I told you — clothes.

DANNY   Show me.

LEONA   No.

DANNY   Show me.

LEONA   Why?

DANNY   Because I want to make sure they're not, you
           know, see-through.

LEONA   There's no bloody see-through things in here.

DANNY   PROVE IT!

LEONA   Don't you believe me?

DANNY   WHAT'S IN THE BAG?

> *LEONA reaches into the bag, pulls out
> winter clothes — snow boots, parka,
> sweaters, clothes that would perfectly fit
> an eight year old girl — and hurls them.*

DANNY   What are you doing, Leo?

LEONA   I don't know.

DANNY   Who are these for?

LEONA   For me. To hang in my closet.

DANNY   Why?

LEONA   I don't want my little girl to be cold in the
           winter.

DANNY   Get a hold of yourself, Leo.

LEONA   I'm fine. I just miss her.

DANNY   *(gently)* Put these in the bag and take them
           back to the store first thing tomorrow
           morning. Okay?

LEONA   No.

DANNY   It's morbid to buy clothes for a dead person.

LEONA   These aren't for Amelia. Not any more.

DANNY   Who are they for?

LEONA   I don't know. The future. They're for the future.

DANNY   What future?

LEONA   We have to believe in a future, Danny.

> *DANNY watches LEONA pick up each article of clothing, fold it carefully then gently put it back in the bag. DEVLIN enters, carrying his suitcase.*

DEVLIN   There's some left over rubber matting so if the ramps need more grip, put the extra down on top. The rubber will ice up quickly and be terrible slippery but don't use salt, use gravel, coarse gravel. *(floundering)* Well, then . . . there's a flight leaving in two hours.

LEONA   *(to DEVLIN)* Where are you going?

DEVLIN   Dan, I should have come round sooner and I'm sorry if I . . . *(turning to LEONA)* Goodbye, Leona.

DANNY   Would you mind putting that suitcase down for a moment?

> *DEVLIN puts the suitcase down.*

DANNY   This place needs a lot of work. We'll have to have ramps build inside the house. Leo wants to plant a garden in the spring. I don't know what she wants to plant — flowers, probably — so you'll need to fix up the backyard, paint the swing, organise the situation.

DEVLIN   Dan, I'd love to stick around and help out but I —

DANNY   I'll even pay you a bit of money.

Silence.

DEVLIN   You've been terrible kind to me, Dan, but I can't stay.

LEONA   Are you on the run, Devlin?

A moment, then DEVLIN picks up his suitcase and exits. Silence.

DANNY   Devlin's a funny guy. Unpredictable.

LEONA   He's on the run from his own this time.

DANNY   Tried to pull a fast one on me but I know this isn't Binky. I'm not blind.

LEONA   Danny, I *(pause, then)* I bought some cream puffs. Do you want one? They were on sale.

DANNY   I lied to you about something.

LEONA   What?

DANNY   We were singing rounds, "Dona Nobis", "Music Alone Shall Live", which is my favourite and "Oh, How Lovely", which is not my favourite any more ever again.

> *Amelia's humming can be heard softly.*

DANNY   We were singing and she was bouncing that stupid balloon around. I told her don't 'cause it might obstruct my view. I wanted to be the perfect dad, perfect father, not a hair out of place, a handsome poppa that never gets angry, never erupts like a volcano.

LEONA   What happened?

DANNY   I reached back to swat the balloon away from her but I missed. I turned and shouted . . . then this terrible crush . . .

> *The sound of a car crash reverberates through him, but much quieter than before, then the humming ceases.*

DANNY   . . . and she didn't die instantly. She kept calling, begging me to help her. She was mewing like a broken kitten and I, I kept saying "Amelia, I love you, I love you" but I was only thinking those words because something was lying against my teeth and I, I . . . I cannot stand that she died thinking I was still mad at her about the balloon.

LEONA   Oh dear.

DANNY   If I could have got to her, Leo, if my legs weren't pinned under the dash which was squished under the car, if if if if, then I heard sirens, paramedics. I heard them screaming for oxygen but I guess when they put the mask on her face she ex, ex, expired.

LEONA exits then enters again carrying the balloon. She holds it in front of him.

LEONA   Could we let the air out?

DANNY   Why?

LEONA   I want to let her go.

DANNY   All right.

Gently, LEONA opens the balloon and a tiny shudder of air escapes. Silence. After a moment, LEONA sits on DANNY's lap.

LEONA   (*singing*) "On wings of a wind o'er the dark rolling sea. Angels are coming to watch o'er thy sleep. Angels are coming to watch over thee. So list to the wind coming over the sea."

Silence.

LEONA   At least we have each other.

DANNY   Yeah.

LEONA   She's in my imagination.

DANNY   Yeah. And the photographs. Always take time for a photograph.

LEONA   Yes.

DANNY   You never know what the future brings.

LEONA   If I had known that afternoon was to be the last time I'd ever see her, I would have paid more attention.

DANNY   We know nothing. We never will.

LEONA   *(closing her eyes)* . . . she wore her hair in a ponytail. Yes, *(smiling)* I remember her hair . . .

>   *In silhouette, AMELIA can be seen lying in a coffin.*

LEONA   . . . and oh, wasn't she one for having everything match — the hair ribbon had to match her socks and god forgive us, but herself had to have black patent shoes . . . and the fight we had over that dress. Do you remember? Do you remember her sailing into the living room wearing that dress Min made — Min and those damned puff sleeves she put on everything — Amelia hated them so. Flatly refused to wear it 'til I told her Min wouldn't give her a birthday present unless she put it on . . . so she did, but with great reservation. I'd resort to that kind of thing only when she was being strong-willed as she was on that particular afternoon. Bragging how she blew up all the balloons by herself, which was an out and out lie because I watched you blow half of them up for her. But so what . . . she felt she'd blown all of them up and isn't that how you should feel on your birthday?

Pause, then remembering.

LEONA   I'd forgotten she'd come back. Oh, Danny, I'd
forgotten. She came back. I'd just gone into
the kitchen to pull out the baking pans when
she rushed back to kiss me goodbye. I kissed
her. Then she asked if she could take one of
the balloons to give to Min. I said yes. I
always said yes to Amelia.

Slowly darkness falls.

fin